The Perishers book 27

By Maurice Dodd & Dennis Collins ● Mirror Books

© 1981 by Mirror Group Newspapers Ltd.
First published in Great Britain in 1981
by Mirror Books Ltd., Athene House,
66/73 Shoe Lane, London EC4P 4AB
for Mirror Group Newspapers Ltd.
Printed and bound in Great Britain by
Unwin Brothers Ltd, The Gresham Press,
Old Woking, Surrey.

ISBN 0 85939 287 2

New readers start here

Established readers (bless you both) may ignore these next few pages of golden words and pass on to the programme proper—returning later to treat the hors d'oeuvre as tasty pickings after the feast.

Or they can do the decent manly thing: form an orderly queue, and go through the whole book in proper sequence from this point on. If they know what's good for them.

It is for the benefit of new readers that much thought has gone into the writing of the following introductions (and even more thought into thinking about the fee) because without them the uninitiated could disappear into the pressed pulp and not be seen for years, by which time they'll be looking like a pressed flower. Or beetle. Take your choice.

To begin at the beginning (oh what a razor-sharp mind this writer possesses) our two main characters are a boy, Wellington, and his dog, Boot.

Sharing joys, hardships, and sometimes socks, they go through life together, Wellington leading and Boot following loyally on. Except that Boot thinks *he's* leading, which sometimes makes for confusion—as illustrated bottom right (I think they were looking for the contract to see if they really have to go through all that's required in the script) but they mostly tread life's trail full of joie-de-vivre; and also full of crisps, sausages, lemonade, boundless curiosity, wild expectations and a jumbo-sized fondness for a wall-to-wall dog, on the one hand, and sausages, sausages, even more sausages, and an overwhelming affection for a hay-haired freckle-strewn shrimp of a kid on the other paw.

Oh, yes, one more thing. Boot thinks he's really not a dog but an eighteenth-century nobleman, transmuted into doggy form by the curse of a gipsy wench. Simple enough to understand. Oh *come on,* pull yourself together—of *course* it is.

New readers grit your teeth and keep going

Now we have Marlon and Maisie—who go together like strawberries and mustard, tripe and toenails, Fortnum and Woolworth, and Morecombe and Foot.

Maisie just naturally follows after Marlon—no matter how fast he runs. On second thoughts, Maisie just *unnaturally* follows after Marlon because Marlon is a lump, possessing a head so packed with bone he has to keep his brain in his boots. This, in unfortunate circumstances, could lead to a nasty demarcation dispute between boot-repairers and brain-surgeons.

This means little to Maisie (it may not mean much to you either but persevere). Maisie feels for Marlon an inexplicable passion of such intensity that the desire of Anthony for Gertrude (a little-known pair of white mice, actually) pales into insigniferance.

Marlon doesn't feel for Maisie at all—no matter *how* close she gets to him.

Marlon may be living proof the human body can operate almost completely on 'automatic' but Maisie is a different kettle of fish, which she closely resembles.

Maisie has an active brain, a cunning mind, a will of iron, sticky sweeties up her knicker-leg, and a voice like a concrete-grater; which gives her the ability to bring nasties whimpering from the woodwork, with a single shriek. When she grows up she's going to be a 'Beautiful an' gifted girl pest-exterminator'.

When Marlon grows up he's going to be a much larger lump.

So far so good and you're ready for the next page. Yes you are—you *are*. You want to be an established reader one day, don't you? Stop snivelling, grit your teeth and keep going.

Somebody call an ambulance for the new readers!

Lastly, but only because he can't run as fast as the others, comes Baby Grumpling. Cuddly (as in 'Hedgehog') little brother and chief-thorn-in-the-flesh to Maisie who has never got over the injustice of asking her mother for a puppy and getting fobbed off with Baby Grumpling instead.

Baby Grumpling views the world through the innocent blue eyes of total anarchy. In order to have the world's problems solved, thinks he, somebody has to first of all cause them. To this task he's applied himself with a devotion beyond the call of duty—and usually beyond the call of Maisie.

Little Grumpling's a child of many accomplishments. Olympic-worm trainer, bathroom-scales greaser, inventor of toast-and-vaseline, the Pollyfilla blancmange, the Wormburger, and an innovation in fast-food—the introduction of carefully placed banana skins to the breakfast scene, thus producing the fastest travelling bowl of cornflakes on record.

He's also an avid reader and a man of letters. Three letters to be precise, C-A-T. He read *War and Peace* in about an hour-and-a-half (illustrating it himself with his very own crayons as he went along) and can bring an interesting point of view to bear on any discussion concerning the novel, since he's convinced it's all about a cat. As are all newspaper headlines, posters, leaflets, notices, road signs—in fact any form of printed word. Now and again he muses upon the grown-up world's preoccupation with cats, and at one time borrowed his Dad's electric shaver to find out what lay beneath it all—to discover, when he'd finished, it was a hairless cat. The Grumpling household is one of the few which has a padlock on an electric shaver and an emergency pullover supply for cats.

This concludes the description of the main characters, but as you pass through the strips you'll soon find yourself involved with a drunken Basset with a penchant for sailors, and, later, an accident-prone duck who's a test-duck in detergent commercials and . . . Oh dear . . . could somebody bring the sal volatile? And a stretcher perhaps . . . .

M285

M286

M287

M288

HEY, BOOT— I'M HOME

IT WAS A SMASHIN' PARTY

AN' I GOT THEM TO GIVE ME A DOGGY-BAG FOR YOU

'JUST HOW BIG *IS* YOUR DOG?' THEY SAID

WHAT'RE YOU DOIN' NOW, MARLON?

CRUMBS— YOU'RE NOT STILL...

— MAKIN' CHRIS'MAS PRESENTS? — IT'S ALL GO I C'N TELL YOU — I DON'T KNOW IF I'LL GET THEM DONE IN TIME

BUT *MARLON*— IT'S COME AN' *GONE* CHRIS'MAS WAS *TWO DAYS* AGO

OH

I *WONDERED* WHAT ALL THE NOISE WAS ABOUT

What *makes* us *grow up*, Wellington?

WELL IT'S ALL OUR GENES AN' STUFF BABY GRUMPLIN'

THEY COMBINE WITH UNCLEAR ACID WHICH RAISES THE CARBOLIC RATE

AN' THIS ACTIVATES THE MOLLY CULAR STRUCTURE AN' THE SHEER *THINGYNESS* OF IT ALL MAKES US GROW

crumbs — if i have to grow up i hope i grow up as smart as you

IT'S NOT EASY

So there's nothing i can do to stop growing up, Wellington?

—'FRAID NOT, BABY GRUMPLIN' —UNLESS YOU SPEND THE REST OF YOUR LIFE IN THE DARK

—THINGS CAN'T GROW WITHOUT LIGHT

IT'S A GOOD JOB YOUNG GRUMPLIN'S GOT SOMEBODY LIKE ME AROUN' TO ADVISE HIM

STILL — WHAT'S THE USE OF HAVIN' BRAINS IF YOU CAN'T USE THEM TO HELP THOSE WHO AREN'T SO GIFTED

KNOCK KNOCK.

WAS IT YOU WHO TOLE BABY GRUMPLIN' TO GO AN' LIVE IN OUR HALL CUPBOARD?

N12

N13

A DAY LIKE THIS MAKES ONE THINK OF THE SHEER *THINGYNESS* OF IT ALL

I MEAN —*WHERETO* AN' *WHEREFORE?*

WHAT *PORTENDS?*

WHAT *SIGNIFIES?*

WOULD YOU SAY THERE'S A *PURPOSE?*

WOULD YOU SAY THERE'S A *MISSION* FOR *US?*

WOULD YOU SAY THERE'S A *PLAN?*

IF I SAID ANYTHING AT ALL, IT WOULD BE *WOOF-WOOF*

THAT'S WHAT *I'M* STUCK WITH, CULLY

HAD I BUT THE GIFT OF SPEECH

IN MY FORMER SHAPE— (OH CURSE THAT GIPSY WENCH) I WAS AN ACCOMPLISHED SPEECHIFIER AS I RECALL

MUCH SOUGHT AFTER FOR THE AFTER-DINNER ORATIONS

GRONFF

SLURP

GRONFF

BURP

MIND YOU— WHAT I'VE LOST IN BRILLIANCE I SEEM TO HAVE GAINED IN... *FLAVOUR*

N20

N21

THINKING BACK ON HENRY V —I DON'T THINK THE SCRIBBLER QUITE PULLED IT OFF

THERE'S THAT RATHER IRRITATING BIT —'I SEE YOU STAND LIKE GREYHOUNDS IN THE SLIPS'

AND THEN THERE'S THAT BIT FROM CAESAR 'CRY HAVOC AND LET LOOSE THE DOGS OF WAR'

GREYHOUNDS? DOGS OF WAR? WELL REALLY

'I SEE YOU STAND LIKE OLD ENGLISH SHEEPDOGS IN THE SLIPS'

—'CRY HAVOC AND LET LOOSE THE OLD ENGLISH SHEEPDOGS OF WAR'

FEET OF CLAY, WILLIE SHAKESPEARE, FEET OF CLAY

ZOUNDS, BUT 'TIS A VEXATION TO BE ENTRAPPED WITHIN THIS HIRSUTE WRAPPING — DENIED THE FACILITY OF SPEECH (OH CURSE THAT GIPSY WENCH)

I WHO COULD GALVANISE AN AUDIENCE WITH BUT A SINGLE WORD

ALL I LACK IS WORDS— I DOUBT I'VE LOST THE TOUCH

WRROWF

JUST TESTING

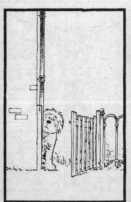

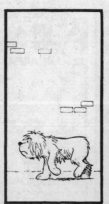

N50

N51

N52

YEUK

WHAT'S THIS?

A SCRUFFY OLE BONE?

WAIT THOUGH

IS IT A PEACE OFFERIN'

FOR THE WAY YOU'VE BEEN BEHAVIN'?

WELL I FORGIVE YOU, YOU DEAR OLE THING

AN' YOU'D BETTER KEEP THE BONE — IT'S NOT A LOT OF GOOD TO ME

BUT IT WAS GOOD THINKIN' FROM A DEAR DIM DOGGIE MIND

IT'S BETTER THINKING THAN YOU *THINK* IT IS, FROM THIS DEAR DIM DOGGIE MIND

N53

DOGS

DOGS

DOGS

DOGS

GS

STRANGE TIMES INDEED WHEN A DOG MUST NEEDS CHOOSE 'TWIXT BUSTING HIS VITALS OR BREAKING THE LAW

N68

N69

BOOT—
HEY, BOOT

Y'KNOW I PAINTED A RED STRIPE ON MAISIE—TO MAKE HER GO FASTER

WELL *SHE* CAME BACK AT *ME* WITH AN AEROSOL CAN— AN' *I* WENT BACK AT *HER* WITH A *BIGGER* AEROSOL CAN AN' THEN MARLON JOINED IN AN'...

N90

...WELL...

...TO CUT A LONG STORY SHORT...

WELLIN'TON— ARE YOU *SURE* YOU HAVEN'T BEEN TRYING TO SELL MY MARLON A BUGGY?

NO—I MEAN—YES— I'M SURE— I *HAVEN'T!*

N91

I HAVE TO *WATCH* YOU, WELLIN'TON, COS MY MARLON'S NOT VERY *BRIGHT*

BUT YOU'RE *CLEVER* AN' *EXPERIENCED* AN' AN' KINDA *WITTY* WITH IT

HOW TRUE —HOW VERY VERY TRUE

COME TO THINK OF IT, KISSY-FACE— YOU COULD EVEN BE CONSIDERED *ATTRACTIVE* BY *SOME* WOMEN

WHAAAT?

NEVER

NO

I MEAN— *LOOK*, URK, YEUK, AARGH

YEA... ON SECOND THOUGHTS

BUT A GIRL HAS TO KEEP HER EYE ON THE MARKET

CRUMBS, BOOT— Y'GET UP IN THE MORNIN' NEVER DREAMIN' OF THE POSSIBLE DISASTERS LAYIN' IN WAIT DURIN' THE DAY

LICK LICK

N94

N95

N98

N99

Panel 1: YOU KNOW, IT MAKES YOU THINK, BOOT— WHAT'S IT ALL ABOUT? / WHERE WILL IT ALL END?

Panel 2: O'COURSE THEN AGAIN IT MAY JUS' MEAN I'M TOO INTROSPECTACLED / YOU WOULDN'T KNOW WHAT THAT MEANS — I'LL HAVE TO EXPLAIN

Panel 3: ON SECOND THOUGHTS I'D BETTER GET THE DICTIONARY

Panel 4: IT MEANS... ER... INTROSPECTACLED... IT MEANS...

Panel 5: WHAT A LIFE — EVEN THE ROTTEN DICTIONARY DOESN'T WORK

N102

Panel 6: THE NOBLE DOG SURVEYS HIS DOMAIN

Panel 7: THE NOBLE DOG SNIFFS A SELECTION OF HIGHLY SIGNIFICANT LOCAL RUBBISH

Panel 8: THE NOBLE DOG CHECKS THE WHEREABOUTS OF A PROMINENT BONE

Panel 9: THE NOBLE DOG SCRATCHES BEHIND THE EAR

Panel 10: THE NOBLE DOG WONDERS WHAT THE HELL'S SUCH A BIG DEAL ABOUT BEING A NOBLE DOG

N103

N108

Panel 1: OH, GET OUTA TH' WAY, WELLIN'TON AN' LET *ME* HAVE A GO AT HIM!

Panel 2: LOOK, MARLON — Y'CAN MAKE AN EGG *STAND* WITH A PIECE OF CHEWIN' GUM BUT YOU CAN'T MAKE AN *EGG-STAND!*

WELL, THAT THERE EGG IS STANDIN' AS MUCH AS ANY STANDIN' EGG *I'VE* SEEN IN A LONG LONG TIME

Panel 3: A STANDIN' EGG IS *NOT* AN *EGG-STAND*

WOT USE IS *THAT* ONE ROTTEN IMMOBILISED EGG WITH A STICKY BOTTOM, TOO?

Panel 4: ALL RIGHT, MAISIE — 'AVE IT YOUR WAY — I DON'T LIKE EGGS ANYWAY

THERE IS *NO* NEED TO *LOSE YOUR TEMPER!*

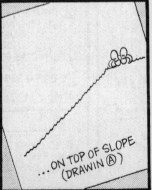

N109

Panel 1: WHAT'RE YOU DOIN' NOW, MARLON?

I'M WORKIN' ON A DO-IT-YOURSELF MANUAL FOR PEOPLE LIKE ME

RIGHT NOW I'M ON SWISS ROLLS

Panel 2: HOW TO MAIK A SWISS ROLL

1. PLACE SUBJECT ~~HURRY~~ ~~HORRI~~ ~~HORYIZONT~~ LENGTHWISE...

(SEE ~~DIAGRAPH Ⓐ~~ DRAWIN

Panel 3: ...ON TOP OF SLOPE (DRAWIN Ⓐ)

Panel 4: YODELL-A-EE-OOOO

—AND PUSH HIM DOWN (DRAWIN Ⓑ)

Panel 5: ARE THERE MANY LIKE YOU ABOUT?

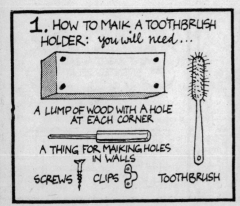
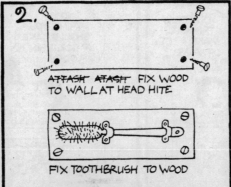

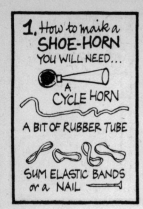

1. How to maik a SHOE-HORN

YOU WILL NEED...

A CYCLE HORN

A BIT OF RUBBER TUBE

SUM ELASTIC BANDS or a NAIL

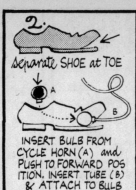

2. separate SHOE at TOE

INSERT BULB FROM CYCLE HORN (A) and PUSH TO FORWARD POSITION, INSERT TUBE (B) & ATTACH TO BULB

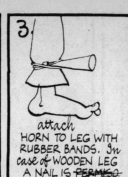

3. attach HORN TO LEG WITH RUBBER BANDS. In case of WOODEN LEG A NAIL IS ~~PERMISO PERMISSI~~ OK

4. INSERT FOOT INTO SHOE AND TUBE INTO HORN

5. when in moshun PRESSURE OF FOOT WILL PRODUCE SOUND TO WARN OTHER PREDESTINONS

HONK

N114

WELL? WHAT D'YOU THINK OF MY IDEAS?

N115

I THINK YOU SHOULD CLEAN UP!

YOU REALLY THINK I'LL MAKE A LOT OF MONEY?

NO — I THINK YOU SHOULD TAKE UP SCRUBBIN' FLOORS

OH, THEY LAUGHED AT EINSTEIN — BUT HE WENT RIGHT AHEAD AN' INVENTED RELATIVES!

YOU'RE *HUNGRY*. IS *THAT* IT — IS *THAT* WHAT ALL THIS RESTLESSNESS HAS BEEN ABOUT?

I'M SORRY BOOT OLE BOY — I FORGOT

I'LL GET SOMETHIN' RIGHT AWAY

WELL HE'S DRAWN THE WRONG CONCLUSION BUT TAKING THE RIGHT ACTION

SCRAPE
SCRAPE
CLINK
SCRAPE

I'M GIVIN' YOU WHATEVER'S LEFT — WE'LL HAVE TO GET SOME MORE SUPPLIES

OOPS

THERE ARE TIMES WHEN IT'S NOT AT ALL BAD BEING A DOG

N130

IT WAS AN *ACCIDENT* — I DROPPED IT DOWN THE SINK — IT WAS AN *ACCIDENT*

AND THERE ARE TIMES WHEN IT'S NOT AT ALL GOOD

N131

OH I SUPPOSE I MIGHT AS WELL — NOT THAT I SEE ANY SENSE IN IT...

BUT IF HE THINKS DOGS SHOULD FETCH STICKS...

AND IF IT MAKES HIM HAPPY...

THEN I'LL FETCH STICKS — CASE OF *NOBLESSE OBLIGE* REALLY

IS THIS SOME KIND OF A JOKE?

N134

N135

N136

N137

KNIFE THROUGH HEAD

JOKERS CORNER

HOURS OF FUN FOR EVERYONE

Matchrite Publications
167 Winchester Road
Bristol BS4 3NJ
Registered in England
No. 2049931

HOT SWEETS

SUPER VALUE JOKES

SQUIRT DOORBELL

STINK BOMBS (3) Will shift any crowd £0.25
CIGARETTE BANGERS (10 in packet) Place in end of cigarette
after a few puffs BANG watch your victim jump. Adults only £0.25
SMOKE TABLETS (2) £0.25
SQUIRT DOORBELL a wet surprise for your visitor,
easy to fix £0.65
BLOOD large bottles of theatrical blood £0.35
BOILS, pair of ripe beauties, with Festering Centre . . . £0.20
WHOOPEE CUSHION when sat on it gives out the most
indescribable noises (best quality) £0.95
LAUGHING BAG. £2.75
VOLCANIC SUGAR £0.20
LUMINOUS SNOT hang from nostril £0.30
SOAP SWEETS, strawberry flavour outside, soap inside.
5 in packet £0.30
TRICK PENCIL it never writes, just wobbles £0.30
MAGIC SNAKE EGGS (6 in pkt) see them grow £0.25
SMOKING MONKEY everyone's favourite £0.35
GARLIC CARAMELS soft centre gives delayed action
(5 in pkt) £0.30
GOOFY DROOPY EYES Jokers TV favourite, spectacles with
goggle eyes attached by springs. Nod your head and your eyes
bounce up and down £1.50
BLACKFACE SOAP Old favourite that never fails £0.30
HOT SWEETS They burn like blazes but are quite harmless
(approx 5) £0.20
DISAPPEARING INK Pour some on a shirt etc. and watch in
amazement as it fades cleanly away. Large bottle £0.25
STINKEROOS insert in end of cigarette (5 in pkt) £0.20
MUCKY PUP old favourite, brown and horrible £0.30
CHEWING GUM with mouse trap action £025

SQURMOLE, furry life like creature with invisible cord, performs
many tricks. Seen on T.V. £0.50
THROW BOMBS when they land BANG! Adults only
(50 in box). £0.55
BLUE MOUTH SWEETS blue centre gives delayed action
(5 in pkt). £0.30
SCRATCHES FOR CARS (2) Almost impossible
to detect from real £0.75
LARGE KNIFE THROUGH HEAD £0.75
RED HOT PEPPER TOFFEES (5) £0.30
OLD MAN RUBBER MASK full overhead mask, superior quality
vinyl, comes complete with grey hair and very wrinkled skin . £7.00
X-RAY SPECS Amazing illusion to see right through everthing,
bones in your hand, yolk in an egg, girls clothes £0.65
TALKING TEETH wind up and they come alive, moving and
chattering away. Best quality as seen on TV. £1.75
MAGIC FUN SPRAY, amazing foam type streamers up to 20ft
long. Press button and cover your friends in seconds, enough for
lots of goes (harmless) £1.75
SET OF DIRTY TEETH Easily slips over your own teeth. This
set of decaying teeth will alter your whole appearance. £0.25
GRABBIT CUSHION £2.75
HAIRY HORROR HAND, full size hand with claw like fingers
and long black nails. Black hair, warts and other blemishes make
this horror very frightening. Slips over own hand like a
glove £1.75
SECRET MARKED CARDS as used by professional gamblers.
magicians. £0.95
DETONATOR, place under book, cushion etc. When disturbed
explodes with a very loud BANG, can be used over and over again.
Comes with a supply of detonators. £0.90

CIGARETTE BANGERS

BLACK FACE SOAP

goofy droopy EYES

STINKEROOS

HAIRY HORROR HAND

VOLCANIC SUGAR

ORDERS OVER £5.50 POST FREE. UNDER £5.50 ADD 35p.
★ *OUR LATEST BUMPER COLOUR CATALOGUE SENT TO YOU FREE WITH EVERY
ORDER, INCLUDES 350 JOKES, SAUCY JOKES, POSTERS, MAGIC TRICKS, BADGES,
AND DETAILS OF OUR JOKE CLUB.*
Send to: Matchrite Publications, 167 Winchester Road, Bristol BS4 3NJ.

CAR Scratch
Moisten with
WATER only.